Photo by Philip Rogers
A scene from the Portland Stage Company production of "The Turn of the Screw." Set design by Judy Gailen.

THE TURN OF THE SCREW

ADAPTED BY
JEFFREY HATCHER

FROM THE STORY BY
HENRY JAMES

DRAMATISTS
PLAY SERVICE
INC.

THE TURN OF THE SCREW
Copyright © 1997, Jeffrey Hatcher

All Rights Reserved

CAUTION: Professionals and amateurs are hereby warned that performance of THE TURN OF THE SCREW is subject to payment of a royalty. It is fully protected under the copyright laws of the United States of America, and of all countries covered by the International Copyright Union (including the Dominion of Canada and the rest of the British Commonwealth), and of all countries covered by the Pan-American Copyright Convention, the Universal Copyright Convention, the Berne Convention, and of all countries with which the United States has reciprocal copyright relations. All rights, including professional/amateur stage rights, motion picture, recitation, lecturing, public reading, radio broadcasting, television, video or sound recording, all other forms of mechanical or electronic reproduction, such as CD-ROM, CD-I, DVD, information storage and retrieval systems and photocopying, and the rights of translation into foreign languages, are strictly reserved. Particular emphasis is placed upon the matter of readings, permission for which must be secured from the Author's agent in writing.

The English language stock and amateur stage performance rights in the United States, its territories, possessions and Canada for THE TURN OF THE SCREW are controlled exclusively by DRAMATISTS PLAY SERVICE, INC., 440 Park Avenue South, New York, NY 10016. No professional or nonprofessional performance of the Play may be given without obtaining in advance the written permission of DRAMATISTS PLAY SERVICE, INC., and paying the requisite fee.

Inquiries concerning all other rights should be addressed to William Morris Agency, LLP, 1325 Avenue of the Americas, 15th Floor, New York, NY 10019. Attn: Jack Tantleff.

SPECIAL NOTE

Anyone receiving permission to produce THE TURN OF THE SCREW is required to give credit to the Author as sole and exclusive Author of the Play on the title page of all programs distributed in connection with performances of the Play and in all instances in which the title of the Play appears for purposes of advertising, publicizing or otherwise exploiting the Play and/or a production thereof. The name of the Author must appear on a separate line, in which no other name appears, immediately beneath the title and in size of type equal to 50% of the size of the largest, most prominent letter used for the title of the Play. No person, firm or entity may receive credit larger or more prominent than that accorded the Author. The following acknowledgments must appear on the title page in all programs distributed in connection with performances of the Play:

Originally workshopped and developed at
Portland Stage Company's 6th Annual Little Festival of the Unexpected.

Originally produced by Portland Stage Company in January 1996,
Greg Leaming, Artistic Director,
Tom Werder, Managing Director.

Originally produced in New York City by Primary Stages Company,
Casey Childs, Artistic Director in March 1999.

SPECIAL NOTE ON SONGS AND RECORDINGS

For performances of copyrighted songs, arrangements or recordings mentioned in this Play, the permission of the copyright owner(s) must be obtained. Other songs, arrangements or recordings may be substituted provided permission from the copyright owner(s) of such songs, arrangements or recordings is obtained; or songs, arrangements or recordings in the public domain may be substituted.

For Greg Leaming

THE TURN OF THE SCREW was first produced in New York by Primary Stages (Casey Childs, Artistic Director) in March 1999. It was directed by Melia Bensussen; the set design was by Christine Jones; the costume design was by Claudia Stephens; the lighting design was by Dan Kotlowitz; the original music and sound design were by David Van Tieghem; and the stage manager was Gretchen Knowlton. The cast was as follows:

THE MAN .... Rocco Sisto
THE WOMAN .... Enid Graham

THE TURN OF THE SCREW received its premiere at the Portland Stage Company (Greg Leaming, Artistic Director; Tom Werder, Managing Director) in Portland, Maine, on January 11, 1996. It was directed by Greg Leaming; the set and costume design were by Judy Gailen; the lighting design was by Dan Kotlowitz; the sound design was by JR Conklin; and the stage manager was Terry T. Terzakis. The cast was as follows:

THE MAN .... Joey L. Golden
THE WOMAN .... Susan Appel

The play was originally workshopped and developed at Portland Stage Company's 6th Annual Little Festival of the Unexpected.

CHARACTERS

THE MAN — Thirties to early fifties. British. He wears a dark three-piece suit. Victorian era. Winged collar and cravat.

THE WOMAN — Twenties or early thirties. British. Attractive. She wears a black Victorian dress. A governess' appearance.

THE SET

Very spare. One Victorian chair placed in a void of darkness. Black and deep green. If stage space allows, a foreshortened staircase and landing may be placed upstage.

PERFORMANCE

During the course of the story, the Man plays many characters — the Uncle, Mrs. Grose, Miles, others. These are indicated in the script. The Woman plays the Governess. There are no costume changes. There are no props.

AUTHOR'S NOTES

When Greg Leaming commissioned me to adapt *The Turn of the Screw* for Portland Stage, we had three specific goals in mind:

1) We wanted to create a dramatic piece that was true to the essence of Henry James' story and themes.

2) We wanted to preserve the ambiguity of the story's point-of-view.

3) We wanted to provide an opportunity for two bravura performances.

We decided early on that the play would be performed on a bare stage without props and cast with just two actors: a woman to play the Governess, and a man to play all the other roles. This decision to avoid a naturalistic depiction of the story killed a lot of birds with one stone. It allowed us to theatricalize the narrative and move it away from "drawing room" adaptation. It also expedited exposition — the Governess could tell her tale directly to the audience, just as her written recollection does in the novella. Most important, it could underline the notorious ambiguity of the original.

It's not giving anything away to note that for over seventy years the major question revolving around *The Turn of the Screw* has been: are the ghosts real, or are they the products of the Governess' repressed imagination? And in a production, you eventually have to deal with a very basic stage question: HOW DO YOU DEPICT THE GHOSTS?

It seemed to us that if we cast flesh and blood actors to play Quint and Jessel — we were implying that the ghosts were real and not products of the Governess' imagination. If the audience could see the ghosts, the ghosts existed. But if we chose *not* to portray ghosts *at all*, we had instead the opportunity to refocus the story as an account being told from the Governess' point of view. We'd hear only her *recollections* of her encounters, see only her *reactions* to the visitations. If the audience couldn't see the ghosts, they couldn't say if they were real or imagined.

Having decided that, other elements fell into place. The woman would play the Governess, and the man would play all the other roles: Mrs. Grose, the housekeeper, the Uncle, and — most important — the little boy, Miles, who is really the Governess' active nemesis in the drama. It would be as if the Governess were relating a story to us and using the other actor, this one man, to help her depict all the characters who were verifiably real. We were also free to dispense with a realistic set — just darkness, a chair, and an abstract staircase to suggest height and danger. We were free to dispense with props — this wasn't a play about lockets and keys and tea cups. And we were able to create a play that would be a tour-de-force for two wonderfully talented actors, which we most certainly had in Susan Appel and Joey L. Golden.

Our goal was to create something rich and theatrical out of something spare and austere, so that by play's end, when the Governess and her demons battle to the death, the audience could be awed not only by what we had done, but what they had imagined.

Keep In Mind

There are no props.

There are no sound effects in the play. Nothing offstage or electronic. The actors provide even this.

There should be no attempt to depict the various locations of the play — the Uncle's house in London, the coach, the tower of Bly, the lake, the garden, the bedrooms, etc. — in a realistic scenic manner. The stage is a dark void that the words, movement, and acting fill. Judy Gailen's original set — with its staircase, Victorian chair and deep green gloom behind — did just that.

There *should* be a shrewd lighting design. The Man must disappear into utter blackness on occasion and reappear just as suddenly, just as he would in the Governess' mind. There is a certain cinematic spook-house quality to this, true, but it is the only concession we should make to stage trickery. I am particularly fond of footlights and looming shadows.

Acting

Each role is a challenge. The Man must suggest a variety of characters — men, women, children — with just his body and voice. But it's a challenge that a splendid actor and a clever director can have a great time with. The Woman must navigate through narration, dialogue, and a state of mind that careens from shy trepidation to headstrong determination to fear, panic, and, finally, a ferocious evangelical fervor. Both roles should be played in a formal presentational style. English accents are necessary.

One Last Riddle

Who is the narrator of *The Turn of the Screw*? Most people might forget that the book has a complicated framing device. It works this way:

1) There is a nameless, omniscient narrator (presumably Henry James) who tells us about a man named "Douglas" who gave him a ghost story to read.

2) There is Douglas himself, whose story was told to him by a woman, "a charming person, ... she was ten years older than I. She was my sister's governess.... I found her at home on my coming down the second summer." The story, Douglas says, was told to him by the governess and then given to him in manuscript form, written in "old faded ink in the most beautiful hand."

3) There is the unnamed governess whose narrative makes up the remaining 95% of the novella (and whose prose style — albeit fevered — is suspiciously similar to that of Henry James).

The novella ends "inside" the governess' manuscript. James never returns to the other two elements of his three-part framing device. (Keep in mind that *The Turn of the Screw* was a serialized novella. By the time James' readers got to the eleventh and final climactic installment they'd most likely forgotten about Douglas and the rest of it long before) Still, I've always been fascinated by who this "Douglas" is. James takes pains to note that the narrative is the tale of a 20-year-old governess who takes charge of a little girl and her 10 year old brother when he is sent down from boarding school one summer. Again, look at what Douglas says: **"... she was ten years older than I. She was my sister's governess.... I found her at home on my coming down the second summer."**

Could "Douglas" be Miles? We never learn Miles and Flora's last name. If so, what does that say about the governess' story? Is any of it true? What did James intend to suggest by such parallels? But if Douglas *isn't* Miles, aren't these parallels rather portentous coincidences? On the other hand, if Miles *is* the uncredited narrator, is he narrating from the grave?

You see the difficulties.

I haven't attempted to answer these nagging questions, but it's in the play for audiences to chew over. Don't make any production decision that firmly sides with either one interpretation or the other. Give the people something to argue about on the way home.

THE TURN OF THE SCREW

After a moment in darkness, a light suddenly comes up on the Man sitting in a chair.

He looks at the audience for a beat.

MAN. *(Slowly, deliberately)* "A ghost story — that tells the tale — of an apparition appearing to a child — always lends the tale a certain 'turn of the screw.' But if *one* child — lends the tale one turn — what then can be said — of *two* children? *(Pause.)* The answer is, of course — *two* children give *two* turns."*(More naturally now.)* The woman was my sister's governess. She was ten years my senior. A very agreeable woman; very *worthy*. *(Out of the darkness we realize a Woman is standing behind the Man, facing U. She turns. Her appearance is composed but anxious.)* She told me the story in the garden. "The *best* stories," she said, "always begin in the garden. A man, a woman, a forbidden fruit; the loss of innocence, the discovery of something altogether ... *not*." The details: a letter, a locket, a riddle, a name. The words are her own — written in her diary in faded ink on the pages of seven days. This is the story she tells. It is a story of terror ... and horror ... and death. It made my very heart — *stop. (The Governess faces the Audience.)*
GOVERNESS. "June 17, 1872."
MAN. "The first day. I meet my Destiny."
GOVERNESS. *(Very energetic.)* The only daughter of a poor country parson, I have come up to London, at the age of 20, in trepidation, to answer in person an advertisement that has already placed me in brief correspondence with a prospective patron, a gentleman of great wealth and stature, a bachelor

in the prime of life in his imposing house on Harley Street! *(The Man plays the Uncle. He stands. The Governess steps forward. Energetic.)* I love children!
UNCLE. *(Deadpan.)* I despise them.
GOVERNESS.   *(Taken aback.)* Oh!
UNCLE.   *(Silkily.)* Not in the flesh of course. *Love* them in the flesh. Despise them *figuratively*, I mean. Figure of speech. In *theory*. As a *concept*. Not my nephew, not my niece. Don't despise them. They're not *concepts*, they're, well, they're actually quite, quite *real*.
GOVERNESS.   I like a real child!
UNCLE.   *(Eyeing her.)* Well, then: this position should be quite your sort of thing! *Real children. Real house.* Gardens and a lake and a housekeeper, all either real or at least imaginative in the appearance thereof. Sherry? *(They look out front. There is no mime.)*
GOVERNESS.   No, thank you.
UNCLE.   Tea then?
GOVERNESS.   Yes, please.
UNCLE.   Sugar?
GOVERNESS.   No.
UNCLE.   Milk?
GOVERNESS.   Yes.
UNCLE.   Quite.
GOVERNESS.   Thanks.
UNCLE.   Now: Business. Background. The house is called Bly, though no one knows why. It is in Essex, for that's where it is. Family place, many years, never go down. Bit like Hamlet's Elsinore: battlements and towers, water below and beneath. Rather a ship at sea, Bly. Very romantic, if that's your bent.
GOVERNESS.   I am a romantic at heart.
UNCLE.   Twelve months ago I was left, by the deaths of my brother and his wife, guardian to my nephew and niece. They are delightful creatures.
GOVERNESS.   I'm sure.
UNCLE.   Never see them. Never go down. It's awkward. I am a bachelor. I have no experience of children.

GOVERNESS. I'm certain you've done everything within your power.
UNCLE. There are no other relations.
GOVERNESS. Re-?
UNCLE. Family. Awkward. Their lives take up all my time.
GOVERNESS. Children.
UNCLE. And my *affairs* take up all my time.
GOVERNESS. I understand.
UNCLE. You *do*?
GOVERNESS. Not enough *time*.
UNCLE. You see the conflict.
GOVERNESS. Persuasively.
UNCLE. I need a woman. I need courage and fineness and a pure heart to guide them. It is a challenge, but the woman I choose must not shrink from that. So many young women, well, they are the very personification of aversion. You're not that, are you? "Aversion"?
GOVERNESS. *(Taken aback.)* A-*what*?
UNCLE. *(Deadpan.)* Aversion. You're not averse to a challenge, are you?
GOVERNESS. *(Realizes, relieved.)* Oh ... no. I *enjoy* a challenge. It's hard to know, sometimes, what's best for a child.
UNCLE. What children want is a mystery.
GOVERNESS. We were *all* children once. What we *want* ... is affection. Love. Protection. There's nothing like a child in pain.
UNCLE. *(Eyeing her carefully.)* The girl is there now, the boy is away at school until the end of term. You will go to Bly then? Immediately? Provided of course that the salary and such are to your satisfaction?
GOVERNESS. I am more than satisfied, sir.
UNCLE. A satisfied woman, our very goal in life. As governess at Bly you will receive all monies from my solicitors. I'll send with you certain *letters*, instructions, that sort of thing. But you — *you* shall be in supreme authority!
GOVERNESS. *(Delighted.)* Oh-*ho!*
UNCLE. By virtue of your ... well, your *virtue*, eh?
GOVERNESS. You make me spin!

UNCLE. *(Change in tone.)* You shall be lonely. You shall be very lonely. Do you fear loneliness?
GOVERNESS. *(Simply.)* I do not fear what I know.
UNCLE. And I should tell you: there have been ... other young women who have sat in this room — gloves on, eyes expectant — for whom the sacrifice appeared to be ... prohibitive.
GOVERNESS. "Prohibitive." It sounds like a plot of heaven. Why prohibitive?
UNCLE. Because of my main condition: *(He takes her hand. She reacts to this.)* That you should never trouble me. *(Beat.)* Never. *Never.* Neither appeal, nor complain, not write about *anything.* You must meet all questions and adversity yourself. From the moment you enter Bly, our communication is "hush." SHHhhhh. Have I seduced you?
GOVERNESS. *(Overcome.)* What ... are their names?
UNCLE. *(Smiles.)* Miles. And Flora.
GOVERNESS. *(Smiles.)* Miles and Flora. *(Beat.)* Miles and Flora. *(Pause.) I do.* I mean, I *will!* I mean, yes, I *promise!* I will sacrifice, and they will be cared for, and it shall be the joy of my life! *(He drops her hand.)*
UNCLE. Success. I *have* seduced you.
GOVERNESS. A question though? The children have been in your care for one year. Am I their *first* governess?
UNCLE. Oh, no. There was a woman.
GOVERNESS. She moved on? *(Beat.)*
UNCLE. She went away. God be with you. *(The Man moves away. The Woman turns D.)*
GOVERNESS. "The 18th of June, 1872. "
MAN. "The second day. I am come to Bly."
GOVERNESS. By the next morning, my heart is beating with expectation. As I prepare for my journey, my head is full of doubts. I have never had charge of children before. I am sure I am not up to the task. I imagine the worst! It is in this state of mind I spend the long hours in the bumping swinging coach that carries me towards my fears.
MAN. Whip-crack. Wheel-rattle.
GOVERNESS. I suppose I had expected, or had dreaded,

something so dreary that what actually greeted me upon turning through the gates was a tremendous surprise! First: the shade of a broad, beech avenue which sweeps up the great lawn past a sparkling blue lake with its own green island shimmering in the sun; above: a looming, Gothic tower over which rooks circled and cawed in the golden sky; and then finally: the great mansion itself, the true splendor of which makes me feel in the instant that I have at last come to life! *(The Man moves D. into the light as Mrs. Grose, a hand held at the side as if clutching a small child.)*
MRS. GROSE. *(Effusive.)* I'm Mrs. Grose, the housekeeper. Welcome to Bly!
GOVERNESS. Thank you, Mrs. Grose, thank you so very much, to be sure. So, this is our new home! Our employer in London did not tell me it was so very bright and beautiful!
MRS. GROSE. The master loves his surprises.
GOVERNESS. It is a *wonder*! I am astonished by its loveliness, I truly am. But: *(She kneels and faces the unseen child.)* But not as astonished as I am by the loveliness of *this* small treasure. You must be *Flora*. Oh, Flora, Flora, you *are* an *angel*. I wonder your good uncle did not make more a point of it to me, lest of course he did not wish to further turn your pretty head! And such a pretty frock and such a beautiful locket round your neck! Oh, we shall be *such* good friends, Flora, sweet Flora, lovely, lovely Flora.
MRS. GROSE. Flora doesn't speak, miss. *(The Governess looks up.)* Surprise!
GOVERNESS. A physiological-?
MRS. GROSE. She simply doesn't. She's ... shy.
GOVERNESS. Well. So am I. That's why we'll be such good companions, Flora. When I was a young girl in my father's parish, I spent many hours alone. If you counted up the hours I probably spent *years* not speaking a word. But in the end I spoke, and spoke a good deal, and speak still I do. And by heavens, yes ... I think I can see a smile, a shy, widening *delightful* smile behind Mrs. Grose's petticoats. Silence is a virtue, Flora. Silence makes a stupid girl wise, and a clever girl a genius.

MRS. GROSE.   She's smiling, miss. She has not smiled for such a long time.
GOVERNESS.   *(Putting out a hand.)* Will you do me the honor, Miss Flora, of showing me our fine, new home? *(A moment. The Governess' hand squeezes.) Success!* I have *seduced* her! *(The Man turns away into the darkness. The Governess faces out front, "Flora's hand" still "held.")* Through the garden Flora leads me to the lake where we find an old rowboat banked amid the reeds, and there at the edge of our small sea we sit on the soft grey wood of our tiny vessel, holding hands under the shade of the great tower of Bly. *(She sits on the stage.)* I am in love with the child. When I was small, I knew no other children. My mother was dead. My father was harsh. Our scant vicarage home was so cramped and dark and ... worthy. I *so* want Flora to love me as I love her. I want — more than life itself — to hold her and protect her. *(After a moment, the Governess begins to sing a lullaby. When it is over, she stands.)* When the sun begins to die away, Flora takes my hand, and as she does she leans down beneath the reeds and plucks such a wildflower — not a buttercup, not a bluebell — but a *nightshade.* We walk back to the house through the darkening gloom, and as we pass under a heavy rush of beech a kingfisher sobs — *(The Man is heard from the gloom.)*
MAN.   *(A sad bird's swoon.)* Oh — Ohhh.
GOVERNESS.   — somewhere over water —
MAN.   Oh — Ohhh.
GOVERNESS.   — like the cry of a broken heart. That night, after we have gone upstairs and put Flora to bed in my room — for I have decreed that Flora and I shall sleep together — Mrs. Grose and I go below to plan the universe. *(The Man moves D. as Mrs. Grose.)*
MRS. GROSE.   Indeed, miss, as you say *again,* a beautiful child indeed. And if you think well of the little lady, well, then, you *will* be carried away by the little gentleman.
GOVERNESS.   That's why I've come — to be carried away. I'm rather easily carried away, I fear.
MRS. GROSE.   Were you carried away in Harley Street? The master. You wouldn't be the first. *(The Governess smiles.)* And

you won't be the last.
GOVERNESS. *(Smile drops.)* The master is a most persuasive presence.
MRS. GROSE. He is.
GOVERNESS. And it is true: he never comes down?
MRS. GROSE. He never came. I'm glad you're here, miss. It's been very lonely all this time, just me and the little baby.
GOVERNESS. Well, the three of us shall make quite a happy little family, I am sure.
MRS. GROSE. As you say, miss — at least until the morning.
GOVERNESS. The morning?
MRS. GROSE. When the coach arrives. Miles. He returns from school tomorrow.
GOVERNESS. But ... I did not expect him till the end of term.
MRS. GROSE. The master sent this letter down with you. *(They do not mime the letter.)*
GOVERNESS. *(Reads.)* "My good women: Expect my nephew by the morning coach. Enclosed please find sealed this missive from his headmaster detailing the situation. Deal with it. But not a word to me." *(Pause.)* Miles has been dismissed — sent down from school. He may not return — ever.
MRS. GROSE. Miss?
GOVERNESS. "... my duty regretfully requires I report Master Miles' behaviors are of a nature injurious to the other children. And hence he must never return to us." *(Beat.)* Mrs. Grose, is Miles ... *imperfect*?
MRS. GROSE. Oh, he's scarce ten years old! One might as well believe ill of the little lady.
GOVERNESS. But — *you've* never known Miles to be ... to be *bad*, have you?
MRS. GROSE. Oh. Well. Yes, indeed, miss, and thank God! A boy who is never bad is no boy for *me!*
GOVERNESS. Oh, yes, I see your meaning! We ... we want a boy with *fire!*
MRS. GROSE. With spirit!
GOVERNESS. We want a boy with fire and spirit! *(Beat.)* Of course, they do use the words "corruption," "contamination,"

and "unspeakable."
MRS. GROSE.   Well, there's spirit and there's *spirit*, miss.
GOVERNESS.   But not to the degree to contaminate, to corrupt —
MRS. GROSE.   Are you afraid he'll corrupt *you?*
GOVERNESS.   Mrs. Grose? The lady who was here before me — Did *she* see anything in the boy that ... wasn't right?
MRS GROSE.   She never said.
GOVERNESS.   Tell me about her.
MRS GROSE.   She was young and pretty. Almost as young and pretty as you.
GOVERNESS.   He seems to like us young and pretty.
MRS. GROSE.   *(Darkly.)* Oh, he did. It was how he liked *all* of them.
GOVERNESS.   The master?
MRS. GROSE.   *(Caught off guard.)* Oh. Why ... yes ... the master.
GOVERNESS.   No, no, wait. You were speaking of someone else, not the master.
MRS. GROSE.   Oh, who else would I be speaking of, miss? There is no other. *(The Governess opens her mouth to speak.)* You were asking about your predecessor, miss. The answer is simple: she wasn't careful.
GOVERNESS.   Did ... she stay here long?
MRS. GROSE.   Long enough. She went away.
GOVERNESS.   "Went away?"
MRS. GROSE.   *(After a beat.)* She died. *(Pause.)*
GOVERNESS.   She was taken ill.
MRS. GROSE.   She went off one night. And then she was dead. Didn't the master *tell* you this?
GOVERNESS.   *(After a beat.)* Of course he did. What ... was the lady's name?
MRS. GROSE.   Jessel. *(She turns.)* It has been a long time since I've said her name. It's late. Welcome to Bly, miss. Lock your door. The house drafts are powerful in the night. *(Mrs. Grose moves U. again. The Governess goes up the staircase, speaking.)*
GOVERNESS.   When I return to my room I find upon my pillow a gift. It is a locket. Flora must have risen in the night

and placed this on my bed. Inside the small cameo are two portraits, painted miniatures. In the dim and by my candlelight I can just make out the faces: the red locks of the female, the deeper crimson of the male. Miles and Flora? By an unknown hand. I kiss their pictures, put the chain around my neck, and turn — *(Gasps.)* What I see before me is a figure of a woman all in black, alone in an island of darkness. We stare at each other ... until I realize it is me. In the corner of the room there is a full-length mirror. I have turned to look at my own body in the glass. My father's house had no mirrors. *(She turns, looking at herself in the "mirror.")* I have never seen the whole of me before.

MAN. Oh-ohh. Oh-ohh.
GOVERNESS. *(Lights change. She looks out front.)* "June 19, 1872."
MAN. *(As Narrator.)* "The third day. The Gentleman returns to Bly."
GOVERNESS. *(Turning to him.)* It is a great pleasure to meet you, Miles. *(The Man becomes Miles.)*
MILES. Thank you, miss. It's very nice to meet you too. Where's Flora?
GOVERNESS. I left her with the housekeeper helping to make your welcoming pudding.
MILES. May I go to her, miss?
GOVERNESS. Yes, you may. I shouldn't wish to keep two such loving siblings apart.
MILES. Thank you.
GOVERNESS. But I do hope that we shall pass many happy hours, Miles. Regardless of what may have transpired at your school, I want to be your friend. You understand, Miles?
MILES. Yes, miss. May I go to Flora now, miss?
GOVERNESS. Yes, Miles, you may.
MILES. Thank you, miss.
GOVERNESS. Miles?
MILES. Miss?
GOVERNESS. Would you like to kiss me? *(Beat.)*
MILES. *Where*, miss? *(The Governess moves to him and kisses his head.)*
GOVERNESS. Go on. Your things will be taken to the

master's room. You're old enough now. *(The Man moves upstage.)* He *is* perfect. *I* shall carry *him* away. Before dinner I take a stroll in the garden of my "Hamlet's Elsinore"— the rooks in the sky, the beeches whispering in the last breeze. I believe I am up to the challenge! I dare say I fancy myself a remarkable young woman! And *someday* this remarkability will be more publicly remarked upon. Someday, sometime soon, *he* will appear and approve — with his light, in his handsome face. I am here to protect and defend his little creatures — *his* children *now*. I have heard stories of masters and governesses before — it is not *unknown* — and there *is* Jane Eyre's success to comfort my improbabilities. This is my magnificent chance! But still I ask myself: What would bring the master here? I am deep within the garden when it comes into view. All the sounds stop. What arrests me on the spot is the sense that my imagination has, in a flash, turned real: he *does* stand there! High up, in the clear twilight, at the very top of the tower a figure stands upon the battlement. But it is not the person I had imagined. I have not seen this face before. We look deep at each other — as if in a mutual *challenge*. Then he slowly changes his place — passing to the opposite corner of the tower. And he is gone. *(Suddenly the Man appears out of the darkness.)*

MAN.   Miss! *(The Governess starts.)*

GOVERNESS.   *(Gasps.)* Oh! *(We realize the Man has become Mrs. Grose. The Governess catches her breath.)* Mrs. Grose…!

MRS. GROSE.   Dinner is served, miss. Is something the matter, miss? *(Pause, as the Governess considers whether to tell Mrs. Grose what has happened. Finally:)*

GOVERNESS.   It's nothing, Mrs. Grose. Let's go to the children.

MRS. GROSE.   Yes, miss. *(Mrs. Grose turns away. The Governess pauses a beat then follows.)*

GOVERNESS.   That night at dinner, I dine at the head of the table, where the mistress sits, Miles and Flora at my side. It is too early to go to bed. Miles? What shall we do? Games? Charades? Do *you* play any instruments? *(The Man becomes Miles.)*

MILES.   The piano, miss.

GOVERNESS.   They taught you that at school, did they?

MILES. No.
GOVERNESS. Then where did you learn to play?
MILES. I learnt it here, miss.
GOVERNESS. *(Realizing.)* Ah.
MILES. Would you like me to play, miss?
GOVERNESS. I would indeed! How about you, Flo —
MILES. *(Interrupting.)* Flora's fond of music, miss, I know what she likes.
GOVERNESS. Well, then! To the nursery we go! *(They move.)* We have not spoken of "the other lady's" departure from their lives, but surely there are feelings there, and I do not believe it right to keep such feelings locked and shuttered. If Miss Jessel had brought music to their lives, well, why lock Miss Jessel away just because she is dead?
MILES. I warn you, miss: I do not play well.
GOVERNESS. Then *I* promise to *listen very badly.* Ah-hah-ha-ha-ha-ha!
MILES. *(Deadpan.)* You're funny, miss. *(Miles sits in the chair and puts his hands on his lap. He does not mime playing the piano, but rather makes the notes of the piano with his voice. It sounds like a talented young person struggling at a piano. The music is Saint-Saens' "Introduction Et Marche Royale Du Lion."* The music" is heard under the dialogue.)*
GOVERNESS. *(Out front.)* His playing is so charming, childlike in its naiveté, adult in its intensity. I understand what happened to Miles at that school. He was simply too fine and fair for that vindictive, horrid, unclean school-world! My eyes stray above Miles' small frame to the nursery window. Rain streaks the panes, caught in the candlelight, like red rivulets, blackness framing the night beyond. And I see him. *(Music changes to Saint-Saens' Danse Macabre."*)* At the window. In the night. It is the same face. He stares deep and hard at me. We recognize each other. But he has not come for me. He is staring at the fingers on the keys. He has come for someone else. *Miles! (The Man as Miles stops "playing.")*

---

* See Special Note on Songs and Recordings on copyright page.

MILES.   Something wrong, miss? *(The Man as Flora claps three times.)*
GOVERNESS.   *(Sharp.)* Stop it, Flora! *(The Man stops.)* Mrs. Grose! *(The Man stands becoming Mrs. Grose.)*
MRS. GROSE.   Yes, miss?
GOVERNESS.   Put the children to bed!
MRS. GROSE.   *(Perplexed.)* Yes, miss. *(The Man moves U., as the Governess paces.)*
GOVERNESS.   *(To audience.)* When the children are safe and away, I tell Mrs. Grose my information. *(To Mrs. Grose.)* Mrs. Grose, we are not alone at Bly.
MRS. GROSE.   Not alone?
GOVERNESS.   Did you see his face too? Looking in through that window?
MRS. GROSE.   A face?
GOVERNESS.   Such an extraordinary looking man!
MRS. GROSE.   You saw a man? Where did he go?
GOVERNESS.   I don't know! The moment I stood he was gone!
MRS. GROSE.   Have you seen him before?
GOVERNESS.   Yes. On the tower. This afternoon.
MRS. GROSE.   You saw a stranger this afternoon? You didn't tell me.
GOVERNESS.   He was on the tower this afternoon, staring down at me. He made his way in, defied me on the spot, and then stole away as he had come. He's a horror!
MRS. GROSE.   A "horror."
GOVERNESS.   *(Defensive.)* I *saw* him.
MRS. GROSE.   Yes, miss.
GOVERNESS.   As I see you.
MRS. GROSE.   Of course, miss.
GOVERNESS.   How did he get in, Mrs. Grose?
MRS. GROSE.   *(Deadpan.)* I have had no opportunity to quiz him, miss. Does he only ... *peep?*
GOVERNESS.   You think I'm making up stories?
MRS. GROSE.   Well, you've had a long day —
GOVERNESS.   Never mind. Go to bed, Mrs. Grose, if you don't believe me.

MRS. GROSE. Miss —
GOVERNESS. I will stay up and watch the children. Goodnight, Mrs. Grose, I'll let you know the next time I see a man who shouldn't be at Bly! *(Governess turns. Mrs. Grose stops her.)*
MRS. GROSE. Miss — Wait. As, as *you* were the one who saw this man — well, describe what he's like? *(Pause.)*
GOVERNESS. He's like nobody. He has red hair, and a pale face, long, good features, rather queer whiskers, red, as red as his hair. His mouth is wide and his lips are thin. And his eyes ... his eyes are sharp, strange, fixed.
MRS. GROSE. *(Hushed.)* Would you call him a gentleman?
GOVERNESS. *(Beat.) No.* No. He's not a gentleman.
MRS. GROSE. Would you call him handsome?
GOVERNESS. *(Beat.)* Yes.
MRS. GROSE. And his dress? Would you call his clothes *good?*
GOVERNESS. *(Suspicious.)* I might. But —
MRS. GROSE. Go on.
GOVERNESS. But they're not his own.
MRS. GROSE. No, they're not.
GOVERNESS. *(Beat.)* What are you trying to say?
MRS. GROSE. They're the master's clothes.
GOVERNESS. You *know* him.
MRS. GROSE. *(In anguish.)* I've been dying to tell you, miss!
GOVERNESS. Well, don't die *before* you tell me. *(Beat.)*
MRS. GROSE. Quint. Peter Quint. I vowed I'd never say his name again. He was the master's valet. When the master was here. When the master left, Quint remained.
GOVERNESS. Alone — with you.
MRS. GROSE. He was "in charge." Oh, he was very clever, miss, very deep. No one could go against Quint. The power he had over that boy. The things that man could do —
GOVERNESS. And yet he was in charge of the children?
MRS. GROSE. The master said as much. It was Quint's own fancy. To play with them, to spoil them. Quint was much too free. He'd put on the Master's finery, and lead Miles off into the garden. "My boy's getting on," he'd laugh, "He's getting

on!" He called himself the boy's "tutor." He to Master Miles, as Miss Jessel was to Flora.
GOVERNESS. Why didn't Miss Jessel separate this creature from the children?
MRS. GROSE. Miss Jessel didn't care.
GOVERNESS. Why in heaven not?
MRS. GROSE. She and Quint, they *did* things.
GOVERNESS. *What* "things"?
MRS. GROSE. Nothing ... nice. *(Pause.)*
GOVERNESS. *(Lightly.)* Tell me.
MRS. GROSE. Miss, there are directions in which for the present I mustn't let myself go.
GOVERNESS. When a woman says she is hesitant to go further, the full distance I fear is her only destination. As for Mr. Quint and his return here, we'll scour the grounds first thing. We'll find this trespasser, and send him packing —
MRS. GROSE. "Trespasser"?
GOVERNESS. — We'll call for the constable on the morrow and have him in irons.
MRS. GROSE. You don't understand, miss.
GOVERNESS. I understand he's a servant who's come back to —
MRS. GROSE. *He went away. (Silence.)*
GOVERNESS. He's dead.
MRS. GROSE. Oh, yes. Mr. Quint is dead.
GOVERNESS. Mrs. Grose: I appreciate the great decency of your not having hitherto spoken, but the time has certainly come to abandon reticence. Tell me the story. How did Quint and Jessel die? What was there between them?
MRS. GROSE. *Everything.* She started a lady, miss. Like you. And he so below. She resisted at first, her Bible like a shield against her breast. But soon ... he did as he wished with her. It was what she desired. A *lady*, done to by the likes of him — wherever he liked, however he liked. They were infamous. Her always calling: "Peter Quint! Peter Quint, you devil!" In the garden. In the nursery. In your room. And the children watching — watching the vile things they did, and saying such horrors, all of them whispering such vile, horrible *words* into

each other's ears. The house hissed like snakes. And then it stopped ... and the house was filled with Jessel's weeping. She drowned herself. In the lake. They found her Bible floating in the reeds. She was better off that way, instead of seeing it through. A woman alone, in her "condition"? You know what they say, miss: The madhouses is full of governesses.
GOVERNESS. And Quint?
MRS. GROSE. It was unnatural. After all her weeping and him paying no mind ... still: when she drowned ... something happened to Quint. He abandoned Miles and Flora, he gave them up. He got drunk every night, in the garden, in the nursery.
GOVERNESS. In my room.
MRS. GROSE. — and then one night — in winter — he dressed in the Master's silks, went off from the house, and never came back. When he was found, he was at the bottom of the tower, not a stone's throw from the lake. The ice was thick on his brow, and those small, fixed eyes were cracked wide open, and his head was split in two from the fall.
GOVERNESS. *(Awed.)* He loved her.
MRS. GROSE. "Love."
GOVERNESS. He loved her after all. Did they who found him call it an accident?
MRS. GROSE. The *magistrate* called it an accident. They who *found* him were Miles and Flora. No one but me knows that, miss. The magistrate thought *I* found Quint, not the little ones. I lied under oath. Oh, miss, you can't have seen Quint!
GOVERNESS. How could I know him then? How could I describe him? Show me a picture! Find one!
MRS. GROSE. There aren't any. They burned them.
GOVERNESS. Who?
MRS. GROSE. The children. After Quint and Jessel died, Miles made Flora take everything and throw them into a fire. That was the last they ever said his name. That was the last Flora ever spoke at all.
GOVERNESS. And that's the story?
MRS. GROSE. You've come at the end of the story.

GOVERNESS. I don't think so. *(Musing.)* Peter Quint. Peter Quint.
MRS. GROSE. What are you going to do?
GOVERNESS. *(Looks at her.)* I?
MRS. GROSE. You are in authority.
GOVERNESS. *(Dawning.)* Yes. The master has given me that. First, the children must not know. We must keep this visitation private. Never a hint. Never. *Never.* Promise, my dear.
MRS. GROSE. I am sworn. And the master. Will you write the master about Quint?
GOVERNESS. *(After a beat.)* No.
MRS. GROSE. Nothing?
GOVERNESS. Not a word. The master is not to be troubled, and we shall not break our vows.
MRS. GROSE. Then I shall stand by you, miss.
GOVERNESS. We shall stand together. Hold me, Mrs. Grose, hold me! God is with us! We must love the children! *(The Man turns away U. and into darkness. The Governess turns to face the audience.)* In bed, I write. I am alone, at the helm of a ship called Bly, moving through the sea at night. If only they knew how afraid I am of water. I am alone, the heroine of their story, and I must see the children safe. I must succeed where other young women — "gloves on, eyes expectant" — would so assuredly fail. The master: though separated, we are really *together*, he and I. We are united in the care of our children. They have nothing but me, and I ... I have them. Peter Quint. Peter Quint. Why are you here, you devil?
MAN. Shhhh....
GOVERNESS. *(Light change. She speaks out front.)* "June 20, 1872."
MAN. *(As Narrator.)* "The fourth day. The Governess at the Lake."
GOVERNESS. At a picnic by the pond this afternoon I plan to question Miles about things past and present. Flora runs off after a black and red butterfly that hovers over the old rowboat moored at the edge of our small sea. I inhale deeply, to gather my courage — and turn to see Miles standing over me. *(The Man stands over her.)*
MILES. Do you think me *bad*?

GOVERNESS. Bad?

MILES. You seemed upset. Last night. Did you think my playing bad?

GOVERNESS. Oh. No, I *adored* your playing, Miles. I had a headache is all. From the strain of reading. In fact: I am today still having trouble with my eyes. Would you care to read *to* me?

MILES. Read?

GOVERNESS. Yes, Miles. I'd like to hear your voice wrapped around my book. What do you say?

MILES. I don't like to say, miss.

GOVERNESS. Are you *troubled*, Miles?

MILES. Not really.

GOVERNESS. Would you like to play?

MILES. I'm too old to play.

GOVERNESS. Ohhh.

MILES. I like a real thing.

GOVERNESS. So do I.

MILES. I like to *spin*.

GOVERNESS. That's not playing?

MILES. I spin for real.

GOVERNESS. Well!

MILES. Would you like to see?

GOVERNESS. I would! *(Beat.)*

MILES. I am not in the spinning mood.

GOVERNESS. You're a *tease*, Miles.

MILES. I have been told that.

GOVERNESS. Where? At school? *(Beat.)* You know, girls aren't sent off to school.

MILES. I know: that's why you're my sister's governess.

GOVERNESS. My father taught me at home. He only let me read the Bible. But I'd sneak in other books — poems — romances. I had to read fast though, because if he found out I was deceiving him, he'd *take* the books before I could finish. Sometimes I'd have to read the last page first just to know how the story ended, in case my book was ... torn to bits or burnt. M*ine* was not a *happy* education. Were *you* very happy at *your* school, Miles?

MILES. I'm happy enough anywhere.
GOVERNESS. You know, *I* can teach you quite a lot, Miles. I can teach you the stars and planets, the seven seas and the five senses —
MILES. *I* already know the five senses: sight, sound, smell, taste, touch! I also know the seven seas, the eight planets, the geography of Eden and where little babies come from. What can *you* teach me? *(Beat.)*
GOVERNESS. Well, I'm sure I'll think of something.
MILES. It doesn't matter. You're *Flora's* tutor, not mine.
GOVERNESS. *(Covering.)* Well. *Flora* is far better behaved than you. *Flora* would *read* to me if I asked.
MILES. If she could *speak*.
GOVERNESS. *Miles.*
MILES. And I would speak if I could read. *(Looks away.)* It's a disease. My eyes don't see the words in the right order. They go all around.
GOVERNESS. But ... if you can't read, then how did you learn to play the piano so beautifully?
MILES. Different. One can learn by listening. And by touching.
GOVERNESS. Well, then. If *you* can't read to *me, I* shall tell *you* stories. But you'll have to trust the teller.
MILES. I trust you.
GOVERNESS. *Do* you?
MILES. My uncle does, so we all must. *(Beat.)* Would *you* like to see my uncle come down, miss?
GOVERNESS. Why, I want whatever your uncle wishes.
MILES. If you wanted him to come, he would. You could write him.
GOVERNESS. I don't think I shall, Miles.
MILES. Well, then — what would *make* him come down? We should think about that. *(Beat.)* Do you like riddles?
GOVERNESS. Why, yes, I do.
MILES. We like riddles too. Would you like to play a game of riddles?
GOVERNESS. Well, I'm not very clever.
MILES. That's all right. *You* start. You're the governess.

GOVERNESS. Well, then: here's one: What most resembles half a red apple?
MILES. *(Immediately.)* The other half.
GOVERNESS. *(Delighted.)* Quite right! How very smart of you, Miles!
MILES. Thank you, miss. Do another.
GOVERNESS. Very well. Why does the ocean get so angry?
MILES. *(Quickly.)* Because it's so often crossed.
GOVERNESS. *(Taken aback.)* Quite right.
MILES. Thank you, miss. Do another.
GOVERNESS. *(Wary.)* Well …
MILES. No, this is fun.
GOVERNESS. *(Sighs.)* Ahh … what was the longest day of Adam's life?
MILES. *(Quickly.)* The one on which there was no Eve.
GOVERNESS. When is a woman duplicated?
MILES. *(Quickly.)* When she's beside herself.
GOVERNESS. What's the best way to keep someone's love?
MILES. Don't return it. *(Beat.)*
GOVERNESS. *(Perturbed.)* Do *you* know any riddles, Miles?
MILES. *(Smiles.)*
    "32 dancers on a red hill
    now they dance now they prance
    now they stand still."
What am I?
GOVERNESS. *(Pause, thinks.)* Teeth.
MILES. Quite right.
GOVERNESS. *(Smiles.) Do another.*
MILES. When is it a good thing to lose your temper?
GOVERNESS. *(Fast.)* When you have a bad one. *Another.*
MILES.
    "One can possess me without seeing me.
    One can carry me without feeling me.
    One can give me without having me."
Give up? A cuckold's horns.
GOVERNESS. *(Beat — shocked.)* Miles. Who taught you a riddle like th-?
MILES. "I am unusual. I have no soul and no body. One

cannot see me, but one can hear me. Only a living being can give me life. I die at the moment I am born." What am I? *(Pause.)*
GOVERNESS. *(Eyes wide.)* A ghost.
MILES. A ghost? No, silly. *Music.*
GOVERNESS. *(After a beat, laughs nervously.)* Oh! Of course!
MILES. One last one: What's *twice* as frightening as a ghost? Give up? Two ghosts. *(The Man looks out. So does the Governess.)*
GOVERNESS. *(To audience.)* It is then I see her. We had been speaking long enough not to notice what little Flora was doing. Flora, my diminutive Ophelia, starting to move into the water through the reeds. On the tiny island in the middle of our sea we had an interested spectator in black and red beckoning to —
MILES. Flor-a!
GOVERNESS. What did Flora see?
MILES. Flor-a!
GOVERNESS. Could it be a woman in black, hair of red, pale as death? Does she wear a locket?
MILES. Flor-a!
GOVERNESS. Could Flora see it?
MILES. Flor-a!
GOVERNESS. Would she cry out?
GOVERNESS/MILES. *FLORA!*
GOVERNESS. Flora turns from the direction of the apparition, her wet petticoats in a white cloud swirl behind her. She stares at me, as if trying to decide which way to go. And then Miles raises his hand — *(Miles raises his hand.)* — and Flora comes back towards us through the reeds. When I have them both hurrying back towards the house, I turn around. Miss Jessel ... was still there. The children safe in bed, I tell Mrs. Grose.
MRS. GROSE. *(Incredulous.)* Miss Jessel?
GOVERNESS. *(Out front.)* Mrs. Grose does not believe me. I *describe* Miss Jessel.
MRS GROSE. *(Crosses herself.) JESSEL.*
GOVERNESS. Mrs. Grose believes me.
MRS GROSE. And the children? *(Pause.)*

GOVERNESS. Well, they didn't say a word, of course, but ...
MRS. GROSE. *You* think they *saw* her.
GOVERNESS. *(Beat.)* I cannot say.
MRS. GROSE. *(Starts to move.)* Then we must question them.
GOVERNESS. *(Pacing.)* No! No, we must not betray our suspicions to Miles and Flora, we must not excite misgivings.
MRS. GROSE. But if they've seen the specters, they must confess their knowledge to us? Is there *any* evidence they glimpsed her form?
GOVERNESS. *(Thinking hard.)* Well ... I'm sure I'm mistaken, but: While Flora moved off into the water ... I could swear Miles tried to distract me.
MRS. GROSE. Why would he want to do that?
GOVERNESS. *(Remembering.)* "What children want is a mystery."
MRS. GROSE. Miss?
GOVERNESS. *(A beat.)* We must learn what these horrors are after. I think I'll stay up a bit longer this evening.
MRS. GROSE. Stay up alone?
GOVERNESS. I'd have difficulty sleeping anyway. I'll be fine. I'll have my candle, a cup of tea and the Good Book to keep me safe.
MRS. GROSE. Yes, miss. As you wish, miss. *(She starts up the steps, stops, turns.)* Miss? It's worse than we imagined — isn't it? *(The Governess returns her stare. Mrs. Grose goes up the steps and disappears into the darkness. The Governess is alone.)*
GOVERNESS. "Midnight. June 21, 1872."
MAN. *(From above.)* "The fifth day. The Lullaby and The Riddle." *(The Governess sits and acts as if she is reading.)*
GOVERNESS. *(Reads.)* "Now the serpent was more subtle than any other beast of the field which the Lord God had made. And he said unto the Woman: Yea, hath God said, Ye shall not eat of the tree in the garden? And the Woman spoke: God hath said, Ye shall not eat of it, neither shall ye touch it, lest ye die —"
MAN. *(From the darkness.)* Creak. Footfall. *(Pause. Governess rises. She goes to the bottom of the steps. She stops. She listens. Fi-*

nally she goes back to the chair and "reads" again.)
GOVERNESS. "And the serpent replied: In the day ye eat thereof the fruit, then your eyes shall be opened, and Ye shall be as Gods, and ye shall know all good and —"
MAN. Footfall. *(Pause. The man begins to hum. It is the lullaby the Governess hummed to Flora. The Governess looks up. Beat. Governess rises. She goes slowly up the steps, looking above her all the while. At the top, she stops. She listens to the melody.)*
GOVERNESS. It is a lullaby. A children's melody in a high, sweet voice behind the nursery door. I reach for my key. *(The Man's humming stops.)*
MAN. Jangle. Dead-bolt. Click. *(Governess takes one step foreword.)*
GOVERNESS. Flora! Flora ... what are you doing in the nursery this time of night? Was that *you* humming? *(The Governess shakes her head as if mirroring Flora's shaking head.)* You shake your head? No? Then who was it? Come away from the window, Flora. Go back to our room. *(Governess watches the unseen Flora go out. Governess looks out front.)* I look out the window. There — below — in the garden, in the moonlight, deep within the nightshade — is *Miles. (Miles appears D. staring up and out front. He begins to spin in place.)* In his white nightclothes. Staring up at the house. Staring up above me. Staring up at the tower where I saw Quint! *(Gasps. Miles stops spinning. He dashes off into darkness. The governess rushes down the top flight of steps.)* By the time I reach his room, Miles is under the sheets — *(Miles appears in another pool of light, this time on the landing. His posture is stiff, his eyes are closed.)* — his eyes closed, breathing heavily, his face flushed and glistening. *(The Governess reaches out to touch him, but hesitates. She pulls away.)* I do not pretend to wake his pretended sleep. *(The pool of light goes off Miles. The Governess begins to descend the lower flight of steps.)* I go into the passageway to descend the stairs below —
MAN. *(Hisses from darkness.)* Sssssssssssssss.
GOVERNESS. *(Stops.)* — and my candle goes out. *(The Governess is frozen on the steps.)* Above me the windows, like cathedral glass, carve a curve of moonlight in the dark. *(The Man whistles a long low note. A long pause. The Governess looks up the steps.)*

Peter Quint? Peter Quint? Is that you, Peter Quint? I can see you. I can stand here in the darkness, for hours. The clock strikes one.
MAN. One.
GOVERNESS. Two.
MAN. One, two.
GOVERNESS. Three.
MAN. One, two, three.
GOVERNESS. The darkness is my friend, Peter Quint. I can see your face in the shadows. It changes shape and expression. Sometimes smiling with your fine, white teeth, other times contorted in a fiendish gash. Can you see the whole of *me* — in my gown upon the stair? My courage knows no bounds. Why is there no one at Bly to witness my boldness? The clock strikes —
MAN. One, two, three, four.
GOVERNESS. Peter Quint! Peter Quint! What do you want here? *(But there is no there. Another sound comes from the darkness.)*
MAN. *(From darkness.)* SHhhhhhhhhhhhhhhhhhhh! Flip. Flip. Flip. Flip. Flip. *(Governess turns and looks down at her chair. A single light illuminates the Governess. She moves to the chair.)*
GOVERNESS. The curious fingers of an unsuspected draft have turned the pages of the Bible and there — written in the margin of Genesis, in the shaken scrawl of a female hand — is a *riddle*:
  "What comes between a man and a woman but allows *everything*?"
  "What comes between a man and a woman … but allows *everything*?"
(From the darkness, we hear the Man.)
MAN. Oh — Ohhh. Oh — Ohhh. Oh — Ohhh. *(Pause, as the Governess slowly sinks into the chair. The Man suddenly appears behind her out of the darkness.)* Miss?
GOVERNESS. *(Shoots up.)* AHHHH! *(The Governess gasps. She squints as if shielding her eyes from light. We realize the Man is Mrs. Grose.)*
MRS. GROSE. Miss, it's past dawn, have you been down here all night? *(The Governess stares at Mrs. Grose.)* You look a fright,

miss, what's the matter? *(Pause.)*
GOVERNESS. We had visitors last night ... and we all got up to meet them. Mrs. Grose, whose Bible is this I have been reading?
MRS. GROSE. *(Crossing herself.)* God Bless Us.
GOVERNESS. And do you recognize the writing?
MRS. GROSE. *(As if reading slowly.)* "What comes between a man and a woman but allows everything?" It's *Jessel's* hand.
GOVERNESS. *(Turns from her.)* They were here. Last night, in the nursery, in the garden. Quint and Jessel. And the children *know*.
MRS. GROSE. They k*now*? But...! Oh, lord, miss, then we must inform the master!
GOVERNESS. What, write to him that his house is haunted and his nephew and niece the prey of devils?
MRS. GROSE. Miss, he ought to *be* here — he ought to help.
GOVERNESS. These spirits have a hold over the children more powerful than they had in life. They beckon to them, and the children come, and then they lie about it. Their uncle will never believe us.
MRS. GROSE. But what do the specters want?
GOVERNESS. If we can answer this riddle — then we'll know what the ghosts desire. I promised to fight for his children alone. The children are in my charge. We shall not write.
MRS. GROSE. *(Tight.)* Yes, miss. We shall not write. *(Mrs. Grose moves away.)*
GOVERNESS. *(To audience.)* But that morning — as if the children had read my mind — Miles begins a chant designed to prick my confidence: *(The Man becomes Miles.)*
MILES. When will uncle come?
GOVERNESS. Miles asks.
MILES. Flora misses him.
GOVERNESS. Flora nods too.
MILES. Write uncle, miss, please, you know how we want him.
GOVERNESS. And later:
MILES. Have you written uncle yet?
GOVERNESS. Asks Miles.

MILES. Flora pines for him.
GOVERNESS. Flora pines too.
MILES. Write uncle, please, miss, it is not too late.
GOVERNESS. And by dark.
MILES. Uncle. Write him. Now. *(Miles sits and "plays" "Danse Macabre."*)*
GOVERNESS. They *know* somehow that I am under the Master's orders not to write. But I will not lose patience nor temper. I don't hate them. I love my innocent babies! I want to protect them, to keep them innocent little children forever! But they're being *tempted* through the garden, and I *must* bring them back! They play. They smile. They laugh — such childlike laughter! Mirthful little Miles, and Flora, the Silent Chuckler! Did *he* teach you how to laugh? What *did* he teach you, Miles? All those evenings in the garden. You're so alone with your secrets. So many mysteries, so many riddles. What do the spirits want? What happened at that school? *"What comes between a man and woman but allows...?"* My head is pounding, and I crave release! And release comes ... and it comes in a rush! *(Miles finishes on a strong note. The Governess turns out front.)* "June 22, 1872."
MAN. "The sixth day. The Tempest."
GOVERNESS. We walk through the graveyard to the chapel Saturday morning to lay flowers for the altar when the young gentleman poses me a question I am unprepared for:
MILES. When, please, miss, am I going back to school? *(Beat.)*
GOVERNESS. You want to go back to school? You're barely here a week, Miles, you haven't even gone to the stable to visit your pony.
MILES. I'm too old for ponies.
GOVERNESS. Really? Don't you *like* being back home? Home with your dear, own sister?
MILES. Oh, yes, I like Flora well enough ... and ... and there's *you* of course, but ... but, well ... I'm "getting on" you see.

---

* See Special Note on Songs and Recordings on copyright page.

35

GOVERNESS. "Getting on."
MILES. And a boy who's getting on shouldn't be so much in the company of ladies. A boy who's getting on wants his own sort.
GOVERNESS. There aren't many *your* sort, Miles. Unless of course dear Flora. You and Flora share so much, so many things I can't even begin to imagine: mysteries, and secrets, and games —
MILES. I'm too old for games.
GOVERNESS. I see. Too old for *some* things, just old enough for *others*? Like ... like going into the garden the other night?
MILES. *(A beat, turns from her, then casually.)* So you *did* see me?
GOVERNESS. Yes, I most certainly *did*. Why were you out there, Miles?
MILES. *(Fixes her with a stare.)* If I tell you ... will you understand?
GOVERNESS. I shall try. *(Pause. Miles smiles sweetly.)*
MILES. I did it so you would think me bad.
GOVERNESS. By going outside after midnight?
MILES. When I'm bad ... I *am* bad.
GOVERNESS. Charming. But how could you be so sure I'd see you?
MILES. I arranged it with Flora. She was to get up and look out the nursery window at me. Flora does anything I tell her. So, you see, it was all in good fun.
GOVERNESS. Yes, I thought it was fun, too. You weren't out there to *meet* someone, were you?
MILES. *(Blinks.)* Who would that be, miss? *(They look deeply at each other. Finally, the Governess turns from him.)*
GOVERNESS. Well, you certainly won't do it again.
MILES. No, not *that* again.
GOVERNESS. Good.
MILES. That was *nothing*.
GOVERNESS. *(Looks at Miles, then starts to move away.)* We must not fall behind Flora and Mrs. Grose —
MILES. *(Asserting himself.)* I do believe I asked you a question, miss: "When am I going back to school?"

GOVERNESS. So much anxiousness in such a little boy.
MILES. A boy has his desires, miss.
GOVERNESS. At the ripe, old age of ten?
MILES. "I am wise in my generation."
GOVERNESS. A quote from scripture, I *am* impressed! Did someone read that to you from her *Bible?*
MILES. *(A fixed stare.) School,* miss: *When am I going back?*
GOVERNESS. *(After a beat.)* Miles: Don't you know *why* you've come home from school early?
MILES. *(Looks off.)* I know my uncle sent a letter down with you.
GOVERNESS. He did.
MILES. What was in that letter, miss? *(Governess moves to change her vantage point.)*
GOVERNESS. Don't *you* know? *(Pause.)* Why would you want to go back to school *now?* Why would you want to leave your lovely home and your own dear sister so very soon? Unless — unless you were *afraid* of something here? Miles, *is* there something ... or some*one* ... at Bly you fear? Is that the *real* reason you want to go back? *(Pause.)*
MILES. You'd like my uncle to come down here, wouldn't you?
GOVERNESS. *(Taken aback.)* What I desire has nothing to do with —
MILES. But you're not allowed to trouble him, are you? Well, what if we could *get* uncle to come down ... without your having to do it? If we could do that ... *then* would you help me to leave Bly? *(Long pause.)*
GOVERNESS. *(Trying to cover her interest.)* How ... would we do this?
MILES. Something could happen. *(Pause.)* Where's Flora?
GOVERNESS. *(Wary.)* Miles —
MILES. Have you seen little Flora?
GOVERNESS. She's up ahead with Mrs. Grose. Miles, what do you mean "something could happen"?
MILES. *(A finger to his lips.)* Shhh. I'll — take care — of everything. *(Miles starts off.)*
GOVERNESS. *Miles! (Miles turns to her.)*

MILES. Miss?
GOVERNESS. Miles, I — I've been wrestling with a question, Miles, one that's been vexing me of late, and you're so ... clever, Miles. It's a riddle. "What comes between a man and a woman, but allows everything?"
MILES. *(A slightly surprised look.)* Why, miss, that's easy. A touch. *(Miles kisses the Governess on the lips. Their kiss holds for a long moment. The Governess' hands rise, tense, then flare out. Miles pulls away, smiles, and goes off into the darkness. Silence. The Governess' hand flies to her lips. She speaks out front.)*
GOVERNESS. *(In a rush.)* Run ... run ... run away! From the church to the park to the garden to the lake to the house to the steps to my room up above! Leave Bly! Immediately! Pack what I need and send for the rest! Leave a note and be done! *(The Governess rushes to the top of the steps.)* I open my bedroom door! *(The Governess looks out front, freezes in her tracks.)* In the fading light I see her. Jessel, my weeping predecessor, standing before me in the gloom. Dishonored and tragic, her haggard beauty and her unutterable woe. Why do *you* weep, you terrible, miserable woman? You have defeated me! I am no heroine! I am alone and unable and *untouched! I cannot save the children, they belong to you and that devil, Peter Quint, Peter Quint!* (The Governess shuts her eyes. Then she opens them. An idea has dawned. She looks to the side.)* Peter Quint. Peter Quint.... Peter Qu ... His Name. *Say His Name. (The Governess looks back out front looking for Miss. Jessel.)* Jessel! *Jessel!* *(Beat. She moves away and down a few steps.)* I must not flee. My governess has given me the clue. I know now how to save the children. *(The Governess goes down the steps. The Man appears and rushes to her.)*
MRS. GROSE. Miss, we was all worried! What happened to you at the church?
GOVERNESS. *(Full of power.)* My dear, I've had my fill of churches. I came back to see a friend. I came back to have a meeting with Miss Jessel.
MRS. GROSE. You *spoke* to her?
GOVERNESS. Well, there's speaking and there's *speaking.* She has shown me the way. I shall not fail the children, nor their uncle. My plot is in place. My gloves are off.

MRS. GROSE.   I don't understand.
GOVERNESS.   I know why the specters have come to Bly, and I know why the children have been trying *to bring them back!*
MRS. GROSE.   "Bring them back"? But the lovely babies have been so good!
GOVERNESS.   The lovely babies *haven't* been good, they've just been *clever*. They've tried to scare me, they've tried to drive me away, they're not mine, they're not ours, they're Q*uint's* and that woman's, and they want to get hold of them.
MRS. GROSE.   But for what?
GOVERNESS.   Miles answered the riddle for me in the graveyard: *What comes between a man and a woman ... but allows everything?* A *touch*. The ghosts want the children, so they can once again touch each other, enter each other, *possess* each other. But they can only possess each other by entering the children and possessing them. The children will lose their souls and become instruments of their vile physic! Miles and Flora can perform their foul deeds *for* them. In the nursery, in the garden, in —
MRS. GROSE.   But what can stop them?
GOVERNESS.   I can. I know how to stop the villains for good and all.
MRS. GROSE.   How?
GOVERNESS.   Hush, Mrs. Grose. SHHHH! I must start from the outer edges of the conspiracy.
MRS. GROSE.   Where do you begin?
GOVERNESS.   With Miles' school, with the crimes his headmaster dared not speak. Why was Miles expelled? Is he stupid? Is he untidy? Is he ill-natured? No. Miles is *exquisite* — so the reason can be only *evil*. And whatever evil he did there, someone taught it him. When I have discovered what crimes Miles committed at that school, I'll have Quint within my grasp. Mrs. Grose, you said the children haven't spoken his name since the day he died, correct?
MRS. GROSE.   That's right, miss.
GOVERNESS.   *(Smiles.)* Where are the children now?
MRS. GROSE.   They're taking their naps —

GOVERNESS.   Good. I need paper and pen. I start by writing their uncle.
MRS. GROSE.   Oh, thank God!
GOVERNESS.   I should have abandoned my restraint long ago. The master must *see*. The master must *witness* what I am to do. *(She "holds" the locket for Mrs. Grose to see.)* This is what we are fighting for, Mrs. Grose. Innocence. Beautiful, untouched innocence. *(Mrs. Grose looks oddly at the Governess. The locket is "shut.")* Give me light for the master's study. My father always said a burning candle was the symbol of flesh and mortality. Let us not burn at both ends. *(Mrs. Grose moves away. The Governess sits to write. As if writing.)* "My dear. Please — forgive — inexperience — foolishness — a parson's girl — condition — your challenge — my adversaries — the children — lovely, lovely — demons — unspeakable — the man! — the woman! — my virtue — your touch — your *touch* — Help us! — Please — the children — save them — the children — save them — our children — come!" *(The Man appears as Miles behind her.)*
MILES.   Your candle's out.
GOVERNESS.   *(Starts.)* Miles! How did you know I was in here?
MILES.   I heard you. You're like a troop of cavalry.
GOVERNESS.   What is it you want, Miles, I have duties to perform.
MILES.   Why did you run away in the churchyard?
GOVERNESS.   I didn't run away. *I stayed. Here* is where the *real challenge* is.
MILES.   Is that a letter you're writing?
GOVERNESS.   Yes. It is.
MILES.   Is it to my uncle? *(Pause.)*
GOVERNESS.   *(Moving to leave.)* Excuse me, Miles, I'm going upstairs to Flora now.
MILES.   You won't find Flora in her room.
GOVERNESS.   *(Stops, turns.)* Where is she, then?
MILES.   I told you: "I'd take care of everything." *(Miles smiles and exits into darkness.)*
GOVERNESS.   *(Turns, panicked.)* Miles? Miles? Mrs. Grose!

Mrs. Grose, is Flora with you? *(Mrs. Grose "enters.")*
MRS. GROSE.   I thought *you* were looking in on her.
GOVERNESS.   He tricked me! She'll be at the lake! Come. *(Out front.)* A storm had come up, the clouds were purple smoke low above the water.
MRS. GROSE.   There she is!
GOVERNESS.   Flora, a short way off, stands before us in the old rowboat. As we arrive, she stoops straight down in her small vessel and — as if she has been waiting for our appearance — plucks the mooring rope with one touch, and we watch as the knot unfurls and the coil snakes around her feet and the boat slides off across the dark waters. The devils know I am afraid of water!
MRS. GROSE.   Flora!
GOVERNESS.   It begins to rain, and Mrs. Grose pitches into the waves, tearing against the reeds, her great petticoats, under which Flora had hid so charmingly just days before, billowing and thrashing, pulling her down beneath the white caps that now rise from the depths, the lightning cracking and splintering above the poor old woman's head!
MRS. GROSE.   *FLORA! (Lights off Mrs. Grose.)*
GOVERNESS.   I look across the banks where *Jessel* stands on her small island, a white harbor in flashing light, the black ocean swirling a maelstrom round her. She isn't staring at Flora in her vessel or Mrs. Grose whose calls are now choked by the sea that disappears her head from view. Jessel is staring up at the house where I know from the tower Quint will be conducting. I look to the lake again, my eyes whipped by the sleet and hail. Mrs. Grose is gone. And Flora's ship is almost to the shore of Jessel's island. *(The Governess closes her eyes.)* Wake up! Wake up! In a moment, I will be out of this nightmare, and I will find I am in my bed, in my father's house, long before Bly, long before my trip to London! No Quint! No Jessel! No Flora or Miles or their uncle! Wake up! *WAKE UP, DAMN YOU! WAKE UP! (Lights on Mrs. Grose.)*
MRS. GROSE.   *(As if emerging from under water.) MISS!*
GOVERNESS.   *(Eyes pop open.)* AHH!
MRS. GROSE.   *(Rushing back to Governess, holding "Flora.")* I've

got her miss. Help me! Come on, miss, give me your hand! Can't you see the child is weeping? *(Pause.)*
GOVERNESS. *(Fierce.)* She isn't *weeping!* She's laughing at me, she's smiling! She'd almost *made* it, why *not* smile? Her smile, her smile, like a flash, like the glitter of a drawn blade!
MRS. GROSE. Cover your ears, Flora!
GOVERNESS. *(Raging.)* You saw her, didn't you, Flora. You saw her *then* and you see her *still!*
MRS. GROSE. You're hurting her, miss, you're hurting the child!
GOVERNESS. Look, Flora, she's still there! Tell us you see her! Tell us you see Miss Jessel!
MRS. GROSE. Miss!
GOVERNESS. It's proof! She is there, I am justified! She is there, I am neither cruel nor mad! She's there, you little unhappy thing! *You see!*
MRS. GROSE. See *what?*
GOVERNESS. She's big as a blazing fire! *Look—!*
MRS. GROSE. She isn't there. Nobody's there. Miss Jessel's dead. The poor girl's dead and buried. *We* know, don't we, Flora? Come along, my sweet, I won't let the Governess harm you anymore. *(Mrs. Grose goes off into the darkness.)*
GOVERNESS. *(Distraught.)* Flora? You leave me, Flora? Here on the shore of our small sea? *(The Governess stares out front, red-eyed.)*
MAN. *(From darkness.)* Drip. Drip. — Oh — Ohhhhh. *(Pause. Finally the Governess rises.)*
GOVERNESS. *(Steeling herself.)* Inside the house. Upstairs I can hear Flora's mocking sobs. *(The Man appears.)*
MRS. GROSE. You can't go in the nursery, miss.
GOVERNESS. She won't see me?
MRS. GROSE. She's afraid of you, miss.
GOVERNESS. She *told* you this?
MRS. GROSE. You and me both know Flora hasn't spoken since the morning she found Quint in the snow.
GOVERNESS. Ah, yes, your great secret. Naughty Mrs. Grose not to tell.
MRS. GROSE. *Miss.* You frightened her. She was playing in

the boat, and the rope let go. Someone should've been watching her is all.
GOVERNESS. She saw the ghosts.
MRS. GROSE. *I* didn't see them, miss.
GOVERNESS. *I did.*
MRS. GROSE. So you've *told* me.
GOVERNESS. I saw Quint, and I saw Miss Jessel! I've described them. How could I know what Quint and Jessel look like? There are no pictures, the children burned them. How could I know?
MRS. GROSE. Look in your locket.
GOVERNESS. Those are portraits of Flora and Miles —
MRS. GROSE. Those are portraits of Quint and Jessel. *(Beat.)* Flora must have kept the locket from Miles. Look at them. You've seen them before. His eyes. Her red hair. It's Quint and Jessel. And as for your "clues" and "riddles" ... Jessel could have written in that Bible *long* ago. It's just the sort of thing she *would* have written — as her *mind* went. *(Beat.)*
GOVERNESS. What a clever bunch. You all want to get rid of me. That what you've got in mind for me now? Speed me on my way? NO. It's *you* who must go.
MRS. GROSE. You're right, miss.
GOVERNESS. And you must take Flora.
MRS. GROSE. I agree, miss.
GOVERNESS. Straight to her uncle. Leave me with Miles. I shall tear out a confession of his schoolyard crimes, then exorcise the devil's name.
MRS. GROSE. I'm taking Miles with me too.
GOVERNESS. I am in charge of the children. Read the master's instructions, of that I'm sure.
MRS. GROSE. I'm not sure of anything but *you.*
GOVERNESS. Be *very* sure of me, Mrs. Grose.
MRS. GROSE. I'm taking them both, miss. You can't stop me.
GOVERNESS. I can, actually. A housekeeper who lied to the magistrate in a court case? That wouldn't go down well for you, would it?
MRS. GROSE. I told you that in confidence, miss.

GOVERNESS. Yes. "Surprise." *(Pause.)*
MRS. GROSE. *(Defeated.)* Miles will stay. I'll take Flora to London.
GOVERNESS. Take the little horror. Get her away. Far from this. Far from *them.*
MRS. GROSE. As far as I can. *(She turns away.)*
GOVERNESS. Mrs. Grose. In spite of everything, do you *believe?*
MRS. GROSE. I believe in the unspeakable.
GOVERNESS. One thing more: My letter must reach the master with you. It's in the study.
MRS. GROSE. There's no letter in the study.
GOVERNESS. I left it there when Miles came in to — *(Stops, smiles.)* Yes. Yes, of course. It doesn't matter. The master will know, despite it all. I'll get it out of Miles, and then he'll come. Miles will confess. If he confesses he's saved. And if he's saved —
MRS. GROSE. Then *you* are?
GOVERNESS. We all are.
MRS. GROSE. God be with you. *(Mrs. Grose moves off into the darkness.)*
GOVERNESS. Within the hour it was midnight, and the carriage containing Flora and Mrs. Grose rolled out of the gates. I went to the master's bedroom ... to wait. *(The Man appears.)*
MAN. *(As Narrator.)* "The Last Day. The Lovers Reunited." *(The Man turns and becomes Miles. The Governess looks at him.)*
GOVERNESS. *(Finally.)* Well. Alone at last.
MILES. *(Meek.)* Is ... is she really awfully ill?
GOVERNESS. Little Flora?
MILES. Who else could be awfully ill?
GOVERNESS. Flora will be better. The spirits here do not agree with her.
MILES. I see. Well. I'm certainly glad things here agree with *me.*
GOVERNESS. I'm so pleased.
MILES. Oh, yes. I've never felt so free. Don't *you* like it?
GOVERNESS. My dear: how could I *help* it? Aside from anything else: there's *your* company. I have *you* all to myself now.

MILES. You've stayed on just for *that?*
GOVERNESS. I stay on as your friend.
MILES. Even though you're afraid of me?
GOVERNESS. I care for you, Miles. There's nothing I wouldn't do for you.
MILES. Then help me to leave Bly.
GOVERNESS. Not until we've finished our lessons, Miles. Not until we've told each other both what we need to know.
MILES. *(A beat.)* Then perhaps I'll stay.
GOVERNESS. You're quite a riddle, Miles. You say you want to go, you say you want to stay: which is it? Who's speaking for you? I think: Miles, like any little boy, wants to go back to his schoolmates. But: *someone else* wants Miles to stay. Am I right, Miles?
MILES. What do you want?
GOVERNESS. I want you to tell me what you did at your school?
MILES. No.
GOVERNESS. They're gone now, Miles. It's different between the two of us. What are you looking out into the garden for, Miles? What can you see in the dark? Do you want to go into the garden again?
MILES. Miss, I'll tell you everything. I'll tell you anything you like, I will tell you, I will, but not now.
GOVERNESS. *(Smirking.)* Why not now, "crocodile tears?"
MILES. I just want ...
GOVERNESS. *What. (Pause.)*
MILES. I want to go to the stable —
GOVERNESS. You do?
MILES. Yes.
GOVERNESS. Do you?
MILES. Yes.
GOVERNESS. Why?
MILES. To see my pony.
GOVERNESS. Liar. *(Pause.)*
MILES. *(Shocked, haughty.)* Miss?
GOVERNESS. I've sent for your uncle. I sent him a letter.
MILES. What did you tell him?

45

GOVERNESS. The truth.
MILES. You know the truth?
GOVERNESS. I know as much as I've seen and heard.
MILES. And you told my uncle?
GOVERNESS. Everything. About Flora. About you. About ... what a good boy you've been —
MILES. *Liar. (Pause.)*
GOVERNESS. You took my letter. You *read* my letter. But *you* can't *read*, who *read* you my letter?
MILES. *(Tense.)* I can make out certain words — like "inexperience," and "children," and "touch."
GOVERNESS. It was you who told Flora to go to the lake. You've been conspiring to deliver Flora into the hands of those *creatures*, haven't you?
MILES. *(Shakes head.)* I told Flora to play at the lake just to scare you, so my uncle would come down and take me away from Bly!
GOVERNESS. Liar, liar, little Miles. Come here, my dear, I want to tell you a riddle.
MILES. I don't want to hear it.
GOVERNESS. But you must, Miles, you're so good at riddles. "What hangs on a man all his life, from the day he's born 'til the day he dies, but never touches him?"
MILES. I don't know.
GOVERNESS. Yes, you do. It's easy. "What hangs on a man all his life, but never touches him?" Say it, Miles! Say it. *(Beat.)*
MILES. *(Low.)* His ... name.
GOVERNESS. *(Smiles.)* Quite right. *His* name. Say his name. Come to me, Miles, I must fight for your soul.
MILES. You're scaring me.
GOVERNESS. Let me touch your face! You're sweating, Miles, the perfect dew on your lovely childish forehead!
MILES. I'm scared, miss!
GOVERNESS. You want to go to the garden, don't you? The best stories always begin in the garden, eh, Miles? A man, a woman, a *serpent? He's* in the garden, isn't he!
MILES. No —! Who —!
GOVERNESS. Touch me, Miles!

MILES. Let me go! *(Miles runs from her.)*
GOVERNESS. *(Following.)* He wants you, Miles, but I want you too!
MILES. Please!
GOVERNESS. *(Grabs him..)* Why did you take the letter, Miles!
MILES. *(Trying to pull away.)* I don't know!
GOVERNESS. Who *told* you to steal the letter?
MILES. No one!
GOVERNESS. Lies again! *(Miles breaks free. The Governess catches him D.C.)* What did you do with my letter? Did you burn it? Is that what you did at school, burn things?
MILES. What?
GOVERNESS. Did you *take* things? *Steal* things? Is that why you can't go back?
MILES. I didn't steal.
GOVERNESS. Then what did you do?
MILES. I —
GOVERNESS. Come on, Miles.
MILES. Please!
GOVERNESS. Tell me, Miles!
MILES. I — *said* things.
GOVERNESS. *Said* things.
MILES. Yes.
GOVERNESS. *Said* them, not *did* them?
MILES. No.
GOVERNESS. And they expelled you for *saying* things?
MILES. For *saying* things I wanted to *do!*
GOVERNESS. Who did you say them to?
MILES. I don't know!
GOVERNESS. Everyone?
MILES. No.
GOVERNESS. Then who?
MILES. I don't remember their names.
GOVERNESS. Were there so many?
MILES. No.
GOVERNESS. Really?
MILES. Just a few.
GOVERNESS. Go on, Miles.

MILES. The ones I *liked*.
GOVERNESS. And they repeated what you said?
MILES. They must have.
GOVERNESS. To whom?
MILES. The ones *they* liked.
GOVERNESS. Treachery! And they told the masters?
MILES. They said the words were bad.
GOVERNESS. The words?
MILES. The words were very bad.
GOVERNESS. But you never *did* anything?
MILES. "Words are worse," he said.
GOVERNESS. Who said!
MILES. "Once they're told —"
GOVERNESS. Who told?
MILES. "Can't take words back," he said.
GOVERNESS. Who taught you that?
MILES. "You can't unlearn, boy."
GOVERNESS. *Say the words, Miles.* What were *those words?*
MILES. They're unspeakable! Don't you see? I'm different. *(Beat.)* I was different from the other boys at school. I frightened them too. I knew things they didn't. I've seen things, I've heard things. I'm more grown up.
GOVERNESS. Where are you looking, Miles? Is it him you see? Outside? In the garden? Hold me, Miles, hold me tight!
MILES. You want me to touch you!
GOVERNESS. Come into the garden! Tell me! Is *he* here?
MILES. No!
GOVERNESS. *He* isn't?
MILES. NO!
GOVERNESS. Then who is?
MILES. There's no one!
GOVERNESS. *Liars die, Miles! (The Governess spins Miles to face out front.)* You see him don't you, Miles, your villainous tutor? Straight before us, see!
MILES. *(A shriek.) HELP!*
GOVERNESS. *(Overlapping, a chant.)* I name the demon, his face in the darkness, red in the night, white damnation! I name the defiler and his power's gone! I hold you! I hold you!

Hold you like my own, my child, so tight, so close! No one can hurt my darling! Not a living soul! No one! God is with *me!* God is with *ME! God is with ME!*
MILES. *(Overlapping.)* Help me! Please! Oh, miss, help me, help me, please, oh, I can't, I can't, help, oh, there, oh, help me, please, please, please, my, my, oh, someone, someone, someone please, *please, PLEASE, PLEASE, PLEASE! (The Governess calls out front, in the clear.)*
GOVERNESS. *(Shouting out front.)* You won't take my child, do you hear? You won't take my child! You coward horror!
MILES. *(Eyes darting.)* Where? Is it? Who?
GOVERNESS. You *know* who it is!
MILES. Is it him?
GOVERNESS. YES! SAY IT! SAY HIS NAME! SAY HIS NAME AND SET YOU FREE! *(Pause.)*
MILES. *(Whisper.)* Peter Quint.
GOVERNESS. *(Exultant.) SAY HIS NAME!*
MILES. *(Low.)* PETER QUINT.
GOVERNESS. *SAY HIS NAME!*
MILES. *(Shouts.)* PETER QUINT!
GOVERNESS. *(Exultant.)* YES! YES! YESSSSSSS!
MILES. *(Vacant.)* You Devil. *(Miles collapses to the floor. The Governess holds him, rocking. She begins to hum the lullaby. He is limp and quiet. After the lullaby is finished:)*
GOVERNESS. Hush…. Hush…. Hush…. SHHhhhhhhhhhhhh. When it is over, I hold my child in my arms — there in the garden — and whisper in his ears everything that has happened in the last six days, in case that he should hear, so that he should know. At last we are alone, and his little heart … dispossessed … stops. *(She kisses his lips. Finally the Governess rises. The lights go out on Miles. Slowly the Governess turns U. Lights rise on the Man now seated in the chair, as at the start of the play. He looks out front.)*
MAN. Of the last events, these things are known: Mrs. Grose died within the year. And little Flora was sent to live in a madhouse, where, as Mrs. Grose said, the corridors are full of governesses. And the lady? After that night, she would only work for families with *two* children. It was her condition. And when

her charges grow too old ... she moves on, like a Flying Dutchman, an ancient mariner upon the sea. She tells her story:
GOVERNESS. *(Turns D.)* We were *all* children once. What we want is affection. Love. Protection. There's nothing like a child in pain.
MAN. Has she seduced you? Well. God be with you. *(Lights dump out.)*

THE END

SCENE DESIGN
"THE TURN OF THE SCREW"
(DESIGNED BY JUDY GAILEN FOR PORTLAND STAGE COMPANY)

NEW PLAYS

★ **THE EXONERATED by Jessica Blank and Erik Jensen.** Six interwoven stories paint a picture of an American criminal justice system gone horribly wrong and six brave souls who persevered to survive it. "The #1 play of the year…intense and deeply affecting…" –*NY Times*. "Riveting. Simple, honest storytelling that demands reflection." –*A.P.* "Artful and moving…pays tribute to the resilience of human hearts and minds." –*Variety*. "Stark…riveting…cunningly orchestrated." –*The New Yorker*. "Hard-hitting, powerful, and socially relevant." –*Hollywood Reporter*. [7M, 3W] ISBN: 0-8222-1946-8

★ **STRING FEVER by Jacquelyn Reingold.** Lily juggles the big issues: turning forty, artificial insemination and the elusive scientific Theory of Everything in this Off-Broadway comedy hit. "Applies the elusive rules of string theory to the conundrums of one woman's love life. Think *Sex and the City* meets *Copenhagen*." –*NY Times*. "A funny offbeat and touching look at relationships…an appealing romantic comedy populated by oddball characters." –*NY Daily News*. "Where kooky, zany, and madcap meet…whimsically winsome." –*NY Magazine*. "STRING FEVER will have audience members happily stringing along." –*TheaterMania.com*. "Reingold's language is surprising, inventive, and unique." –*nytheatre.com*. "…[a] whimsical comic voice." –*Time Out*. [3M, 3W (doubling)] ISBN: 0-8222-1952-2

★ **DEBBIE DOES DALLAS adapted by Erica Schmidt, composed by Andrew Sherman, conceived by Susan L. Schwartz.** A modern morality tale told as a comic musical of tragic proportions as the classic film is brought to the stage. "A scream! A saucy, tongue-in-cheek romp." –*The New Yorker*. "Hilarious! DEBBIE manages to have it all: beauty, brains and a great sense of humor!" –*Time Out*. "Shamelessly silly, shrewdly self-aware and proud of being naughty. Great fun!" –*NY Times*. "Racy and raucous, a lighthearted, fast-paced thoroughly engaging and hilarious send-up." –*NY Daily News*. [3M, 5W] ISBN: 0-8222-1955-7

★ **THE MYSTERY PLAYS by Roberto Aguirre-Sacasa.** Two interrelated one acts, loosely based on the tradition of the medieval mystery plays. "… stylish, spine-tingling…Mr. Aguirre-Sacasa uses standard tricks of horror stories, borrowing liberally from masters like Kafka Lovecraft, Hitchcock…But his mastery of the genre is his own…irresistible." –*NY Times*. "Undaunted by the special-effects limitations of theatre, playwright and *Marvel* comicbook writer Roberto Aguirre-Sacasa maps out some creepy twilight zones in THE MYSTERY PLAYS, an engaging, related pair of one acts…The theatre may rarely deliver shocks equivalent to, say, *Dawn of the Dead*, but Aguirre-Sacasa's work is fine compensation." –*Time Out*. [4M, 2W] ISBN: 0-8222-2038-5

★ **THE JOURNALS OF MIHAIL SEBASTIAN by David Auburn.** This epic one-man play spans eight tumultuous years and opens a uniquely personal window on the Romanian Holocaust and the Second World War. "Powerful." –*NY Times*. "[THE JOURNALS OF MIHAIL SEBASTIAN] allows us to glimpse the idiosyncratic effects of that awful history on one intelligent, pragmatic, recognizably real man…" –*NY Newsday*. [3M, 5W] ISBN: 0-8222-2006-7

★ **LIVING OUT by Lisa Loomer.** The story of the complicated relationship between a Salvadoran nanny and the Anglo lawyer she works for. "A stellar new play. Searingly funny." –*The New Yorker*. "Both generous and merciless, equally enjoyable and disturbing." –*NY Newsday*. "A bitingly funny new comedy. The plight of working mothers is explored from two pointedly contrasting perspectives in this sympathetic, sensitive new play." –*Variety*. [2M, 6W] ISBN: 0-8222-1994-8

DRAMATISTS PLAY SERVICE, INC.
440 Park Avenue South, New York, NY 10016 212-683-8960 Fax 212-213-1539
postmaster@dramatists.com   www.dramatists.com

NEW PLAYS

★ **MATCH by Stephen Belber.** Mike and Lisa Davis interview a dancer and choreographer about his life, but it is soon evident that their agenda will either ruin or inspire them—and definitely change their lives forever. "Prolific laughs and ear-to-ear smiles." –*NY Magazine*. "Uproariously funny, deeply moving, enthralling theater. Stephen Belber's MATCH has great beauty and tenderness, and abounds in wit." –*NY Daily News*. "Three and a half out of four stars." –*USA Today*. "A theatrical steeplechase that leads straight from outrageous bitchery to unadorned, heartfelt emotion." –*Wall Street Journal*. [2M, 1W] ISBN: 0-8222-2020-2

★ **HANK WILLIAMS: LOST HIGHWAY by Randal Myler and Mark Harelik.** The story of the beloved and volatile country-music legend Hank Williams, featuring twenty-five of his most unforgettable songs. "[LOST HIGHWAY has] the exhilarating feeling of Williams on stage in a particular place on a particular night…serves up classic country with the edges raw and the energy hot…By the end of the play, you've traveled on a profound emotional journey: LOST HIGHWAY transports its audience and communicates the inspiring message of the beauty and richness of Williams' songs…forceful, clear-eyed, moving, impressive." –*Rolling Stone*. "…honors a very particular musical talent with care and energy… smart, sweet, poignant." –*NY Times*. [7M, 3W] ISBN: 0-8222-1985-9

★ **THE STORY by Tracey Scott Wilson.** An ambitious black newspaper reporter goes against her editor to investigate a murder and finds the *best* story…but at what cost? "A singular new voice…deeply emotional, deeply intellectual, and deeply musical…" –*The New Yorker*. "…a conscientious and absorbing new drama…" –*NY Times*. "…a riveting, tough-minded drama about race, reporting and the truth…" –*A.P.* "… a stylish, attention-holding script that ends on a chilling note that will leave viewers with much to talk about." –*Curtain Up*. [2M, 7W (doubling, flexible casting)] ISBN: 0-8222-1998-0

★ **OUR LADY OF 121st STREET by Stephen Adly Guirgis.** The body of Sister Rose, beloved Harlem nun, has been stolen, reuniting a group of life-challenged childhood friends who square off as they wait for her return. "A scorching and dark new comedy… Mr. Guirgis has one of the finest imaginations for dialogue to come along in years." –*NY Times*. "Stephen Guirgis may be the best playwright in America under forty." –*NY Magazine*. [8M, 4W] ISBN: 0-8222-1965-4

★ **HOLLYWOOD ARMS by Carrie Hamilton and Carol Burnett.** The coming-of-age story of a dreamer who manages to escape her bleak life and follow her romantic ambitions to stardom. Based on Carol Burnett's bestselling autobiography, *One More Time*. "…pure theatre and pure entertainment…" –*Talkin' Broadway*. "…a warm, fuzzy evening of theatre." –*BrodwayBeat.com*. "…chuckles and smiles of recognition or surprise flow naturally…a remarkable slice of life." –*TheatreScene.net*. [5M, 5W, 1 girl] ISBN: 0-8222-1959-X

★ **INVENTING VAN GOGH by Steven Dietz.** A haunting and hallucinatory drama about the making of art, the obsession to create and the fine line that separates truth from myth. "Like a van Gogh painting, Dietz's story is a gorgeous example of excess—one that remakes reality with broad, well-chosen brush strokes. At evening's end, we're left with the author's resounding opinions on art and artifice, and provoked by his constant query into which is greater: van Gogh's art or his violent myth." –*Phoenix New Times*. "Dietz's writing is never simple. It is always brilliant. Shaded, compressed, direct, lucid—he frames his subject with a remarkable understanding of painting as a physical experience." –*Tucson Citizen*. [4M, 1W] ISBN: 0-8222-1954-9

DRAMATISTS PLAY SERVICE, INC.
440 Park Avenue South, New York, NY 10016 212-683-8960 Fax 212-213-1539
postmaster@dramatists.com   www.dramatists.com

NEW PLAYS

★ **INTIMATE APPAREL by Lynn Nottage.** The moving and lyrical story of a turn-of-the-century black seamstress whose gifted hands and sewing machine are the tools she uses to fashion her dreams from the whole cloth of her life's experiences. "…Nottage's play has a delicacy and eloquence that seem absolutely right for the time she is depicting…" –*NY Daily News*. "…thoughtful, affecting…The play offers poignant commentary on an era when the cut and color of one's dress—and of course, skin—determined whom one could and could not marry, sleep with, even talk to in public." –*Variety*. [2M, 4W] ISBN: 0-8222-2009-1

★ **BROOKLYN BOY by Donald Margulies.** A witty and insightful look at what happens to a writer when his novel hits the bestseller list. "The characters are beautifully drawn, the dialogue sparkles…" –*nytheatre.com*. "Few playwrights have the mastery to smartly investigate so much through a laugh-out-loud comedy that combines the vintage subject matter of successful writer-returning-to-ethnic-roots with the familiar mid-life crisis." –*Show Business Weekly*. [4M, 3W] ISBN: 0-8222-2074-1

★ **CROWNS by Regina Taylor.** Hats become a springboard for an exploration of black history and identity in this celebratory musical play. "Taylor pulls off a Hat Trick: She scores thrice, turning CROWNS into an artful amalgamation of oral history, fashion show, and musical theater…" –*TheatreMania.com*. "…wholly theatrical…Ms. Taylor has created a show that seems to arise out of spontaneous combustion, as if a bevy of department-store customers simultaneously decided to stage a revival meeting in the changing room." –*NY Times*. [1M, 6W (2 musicians)] ISBN: 0-8222-1963-8

★ **EXITS AND ENTRANCES by Athol Fugard.** The story of a relationship between a young playwright on the threshold of his career and an aging actor who has reached the end of his "[Fugard] can say more with a single line than most playwrights convey in an entire script…Paraphrasing the title, it's safe to say this drama, making its memorable entrance into our consciousness, is unlikely to exit as long as a theater exists for exceptional work." –*Variety*. "A thought-provoking, elegant and engrossing new play…" –*Hollywood Reporter*. [2M] ISBN: 0-8222-2041-5

★ **BUG by Tracy Letts.** A thriller featuring a pair of star-crossed lovers in an Oklahoma City motel facing a bug invasion, paranoia, conspiracy theories and twisted psychological motives. "…obscenely exciting…top-flight craftsmanship. Buckle up and brace yourself…" –*NY Times*. "…[a] thoroughly outrageous and thoroughly entertaining play…the possibility of enemies, real and imagined, to squash has never been more theatrical." –*A.P.* [3M, 2W] ISBN: 0-8222-2016-4

★ **THOM PAIN (BASED ON NOTHING) by Will Eno.** An ordinary man muses on childhood, yearning, disappointment and loss, as he draws the audience into his last-ditch plea for empathy and enlightenment. "It's one of those treasured nights in the theater—treasured nights anywhere, for that matter—that can leave you both breathless with exhilaration and…in a puddle of tears." –*NY Times*. "Eno's words…are familiar, but proffered in a way that is constantly contradictory to our expectations. Beckett is certainly among his literary ancestors." –*nytheatre.com*. [1M] ISBN: 0-8222-2076-8

★ **THE LONG CHRISTMAS RIDE HOME by Paula Vogel.** Past, present and future collide on a snowy Christmas Eve for a troubled family of five. "…[a] lovely and hauntingly original family drama…a work that breathes so much life into the theater." –*Time Out*. "…[a] delicate visual feast…" –*NY Times*. "…brutal and lovely…the overall effect is magical." –*NY Newsday*. [3M, 3W] ISBN: 0-8222-2003-2

DRAMATISTS PLAY SERVICE, INC.
440 Park Avenue South, New York, NY 10016 212-683-8960 Fax 212-213-1539
postmaster@dramatists.com www.dramatists.com